poultry in motion

D0801518

Man is
the only animal
that blushes.
Or needs to.

Mark Twain

this book belongs to

o o o o o o o o o o o o o o o o

o o o o o o o o o o o o o o o o o

o o o o o o o o o o o o o o o o

SHEEPWRECK

SIMON DREW'S
BEASTLY
ADDRESS BOOK

FOR BEASTLY FRIENDS

Antique Collectors' Club

First published 1993

© Simon Drew

ISBN 1 85149 188 0

Printed on Consort Royal Satin from Donside Mills, Aberdeen

Published in England by the Antique Collectors' Club Ltd., Woodbridge, Suffolk IP12 1DS

Foreword

I was asked to do a foreword for this book and said it would be a piece of cake.

s.d.

Art

name	name
address	address
telephone	telephone
fax	fax

...and here's one I painted earlier.

name

address

telephone

fax

name

address

telephone

fax

name

address

telephone

fax

name

address

telephone

fax

name

address

telephone

fax

name

address

telephone

fax

Armadillo

name ....

address ....

....

....

telephone ....

fax ....

name ....

address ....

....

....

telephone ....

fax ....

name ....

address ....

....

....

telephone ....

fax ....

name ....

address ....

....

....

telephone ....

fax ....

if you sleep under blankets patterned with stripes
with your nose sticking out from the pillow
a passing zoologist might say you are
a five-banded (dead) armadillo.

name

address

telephone

fax

name

address

telephone

fax

name

address

telephone

fax

name

address

telephone

fax

name

address

telephone

fax

name

address

telephone

fax

Aardvark

name

address

telephone

fax

name

address

telephone

fax

name

address

telephone

fax

name

address

telephone

fax

name

address

telephone

fax

name

address

telephone

fax

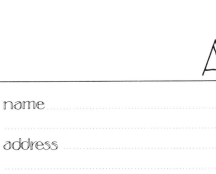

great mistakes of history:
the trojan aardvark

name.................................

address.................................

....

telephone.................................

fax.................................

name.................................

address.................................

....

telephone.................................

fax.................................

name.................................

address.................................

....

telephone.................................

fax.................................

name.................................

address.................................

....

telephone.................................

fax.................................

Bureaucat

name

address

telephone

fax

name

address

telephone

fax

name

address

telephone

fax

name

address

telephone

fax

name

address

telephone

fax

name

address

telephone

fax

name

address

telephone

fax

name

address

telephone

fax

name

address

telephone

fax

name

address

telephone

fax

name

address

telephone

fax

bureaucat

Bird

name

address

telephone

fax

name

address

telephone

fax

name

address

telephone

fax

name

address

telephone

fax

name

address

telephone

fax

name

address

telephone

fax

BIRD DROPPING

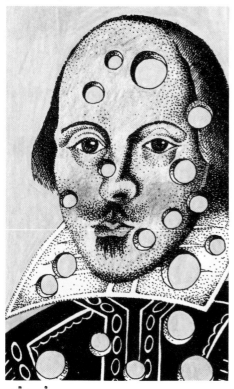

shakespeare
with holes

name

address

telephone

fox

---

name

address

telephone

fox

---

name

address

telephone

fox

---

name

address

telephone

fox

name

address

telephone

fax

name

address

telephone

fax

no holes bard

name

address

telephone

fax

name

address

telephone

fax

Cat

name

address

telephone

fax

name

address

telephone

fax

name

address

telephone

fax

name

address

telephone

fax

name

address

telephone

fax

name

address

telephone

fax

cat with piano tuna

name ....

address ....

....

telephone ....

fax ....

name ....

address ....

....

telephone ....

fax ....

Cod

name

address

telephone

fax

---

name

address

telephone

fax

---

name

address

telephone

fax

---

name

address

telephone

fax

---

name

address

telephone

fax

---

name

address

telephone

fax

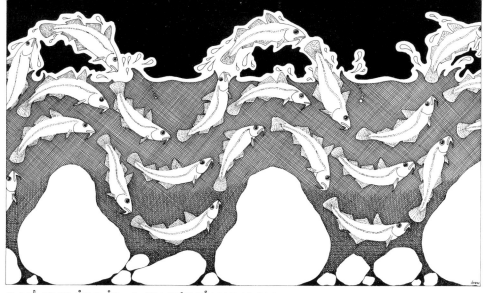

cod moving in a mysterious way

name

address

telephone

fax

name

address

telephone

fax

name

address

telephone

fax

name

address

telephone

fax

C

name

address

telephone

fax

---

name

address

telephone

fax

---

name

address

telephone

fax

---

name

address

telephone

fax

---

name

address

telephone

fax

---

name

address

telephone

fax

C

cat with open toad sandal

Duck

name

address

telephone

fax

name

address

telephone

fax

name

address

telephone

fax

name

address

telephone

fax

name

address

telephone

fax

name

address

telephone

fax

DUCK

name

address

telephone

fax

name

address

telephone

fax

name

address

telephone

fax

name

address

telephone

fax

name

address

telephone

fax

name ....

address ....

....

....

telephone ....

fax ....

name ....

address ....

....

....

telephone ....

fax ....

name ....

address ....

....

....

telephone ....

fax ....

name

address

telephone

fax

name

address

telephone

fax

name

address

telephone

fax

D

name

address

telephone

fax

name

address

telephone

fax

name

address

telephone

fax

name

address

telephone

fax

name

address

telephone

fax

name

address

telephone

fax

name

address

telephone

fax

---

name

address

telephone

fax

---

name

address

telephone

fax

---

name

address

telephone

fax

---

name

address

telephone

fax

---

name

address

telephone

fax

Emu

name		name	
address		address	
telephone		telephone	
fax		fax	

name		name	
address		address	
telephone		telephone	
fax		fax	

name		name	
address		address	
telephone		telephone	
fax		fax	

....and when there are emus in blazers and boaters whose kneecaps are fitted with powerful motors....

Egg

name ....

address ....

....

....

telephone ....

fax ....

because a
bird has no
placenta
eggs is how
this world
they enter

---

name ....

address ....

....

....

telephone ....

fax ....

name ....

address ....

....

....

telephone ....

fax ....

---

name ....

address ....

....

....

telephone ....

fax ....

name ....

address ....

....

....

telephone ....

fax ....

Eider

name

address

telephone

fax

---

name

address

telephone

fax

---

name

address

telephone

fax

---

name

address

telephone

fax

EIDER WAY UP

EIDER WAY UP

Fish

name ....

address ....
....
....

telephone ....

fax ....

name ....

address ....
....
....

telephone ....

fax ....

name ....

address ....
....
....

telephone ....

fax ....

name ....

address ....
....
....

telephone ....

fax ....

name ....

address ....
....
....

telephone ....

fax ....

name ....

address ....
....
....

telephone ....

fax ....

F

hear no fish,
see no fish,
speak no fish

F

name

address

telephone

fax

name

address

telephone

fax

name

address

telephone

fax

name

address

telephone

fax

name

address

telephone

fax

name

address

telephone

fax

name

address

telephone

fax

name

address

telephone

fax

name

address

telephone

fax

name

address

telephone

fax

name

address

telephone

fax

name

address

telephone

fax

Fish

name ....

address ....

....

....

telephone ....

fax ....

name ....

address ....

....

....

telephone ....

fax ....

name ....

address ....

....

....

telephone ....

fax ....

name ....

address ....

....

....

telephone ....

fax ....

name ....

address ....

....

....

telephone ....

fax ....

name ....

address ....

....

....

telephone ....

fax ....

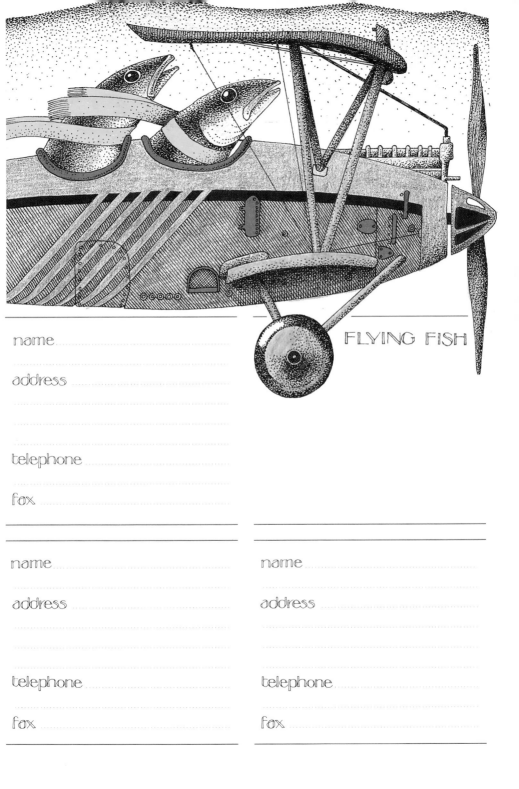

FLYING FISH

name

address

telephone

fax

name

address

telephone

fax

name

address

telephone

fax

Gannet

name ....

address ....

....

....

telephone ....

fax ....

---

name ....

address ....

....

....

telephone ....

fax ....

---

name ....

address ....

....

....

telephone ....

fax ....

---

name ....

address ....

....

....

telephone ....

fax ....

---

name ....

address ....

....

....

telephone ....

fax ....

---

name ....

address ....

....

....

telephone ....

fax ....

the wily gannet sits on granite
thus avoiding germs
and so this bird must feed on fish
for granite has no worms.

name.....................................

address.................................

....

....

telephone.............................

fax..

---

name.....................................

address.................................

....

....

telephone.............................

fax..

---

name.....................................

address.................................

....

....

telephone.............................

fax..

---

name.....................................

address.................................

....

....

telephone.............................

fax..

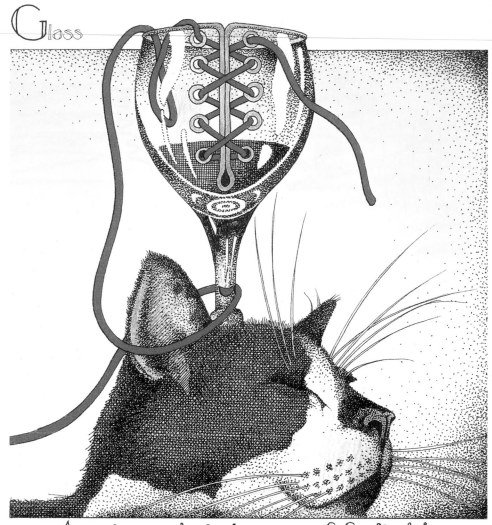

A cat carried glasses of fruit juice
despite never liking the taste,
but while he was sleeping
his friends entered creeping
on dastardly missions,
and little additions
were made to the juices,
with silent excuses.
(The drink in this picture is laced.)

name

address

telephone

fax

name

address

telephone

fax

name

address

telephone

fax

name

address

telephone

fax

name

address

telephone

fax

name

address

telephone

fax

name

address

telephone

fax

name

address

telephone

fax

name

address

telephone

fax

name

address

telephone

fax

name

address

telephone

fax

name

address

telephone

fax

name

address

telephone

fax

name

address

telephone

fax

name

address

telephone

fax

name

address

telephone

fax

name

address

telephone

fax

name

address

telephone

fax

Hares

name

address

telephone

fax

---

name

address

telephone

fax

---

name

address

telephone

fax

---

name

address

telephone

fax

---

name

address

telephone

fax

---

name

address

telephone

fax

hares and graces

a slug in a salad is rather a fright;
a fly in your tea is a miserable sight;
but one of the things that I utterly hate
is finding a hare on the side of my plate.

name..

address ....

....

....

telephone..

fax ....

name..

address ....

....

....

telephone..

fax ....

H

name ....

address ....

....

....

telephone ....

fax ....

name ....

address ....

....

....

telephone ....

fax ....

name ....

address ....

....

....

telephone ....

fax ....

name ....

address ....

....

....

telephone ....

fax ....

name ....

address ....

....

....

telephone ....

fax ....

name ....

address ....

....

....

telephone ....

fax ....

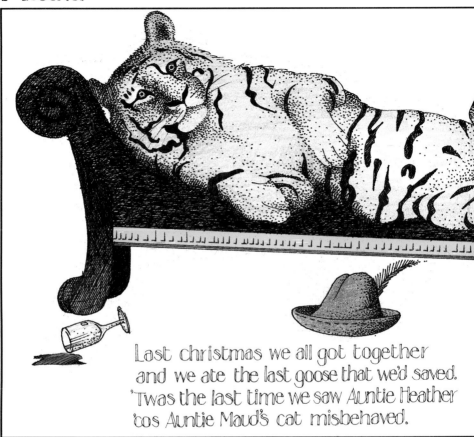

Last christmas we all got together
and we ate the last goose that we'd saved.
'Twas the last time we saw Auntie Heather
'cos Auntie Maud's cat misbehaved.

name

address

telephone

fax

name

address

telephone

fax

H

name

address

telephone

fax

name

address

telephone

fax

name

address

telephone

fax

name

address

telephone

fax

name

address

telephone

fax

name

address

telephone

fax

Idol

a camel attempting
to pass through the knee of an idol.

name
address

telephone
fax

name
address

telephone
fax

name
address

telephone
fax

name
address

telephone
fax

name

address

telephone

fax

name

address

telephone

fax

name

address

telephone

fax

name

address

telephone

fax

name

address

telephone

fax

name

address

telephone

fax

I for eyes

drew

'Of course, the sign of a really good painting is when they follow you round the room.'

name ....

address ....

....

....

telephone ....

fax ....

name ....

address ....

....

....

telephone ....

fax ....

I

name

address

telephone

fax

name

address

telephone

fax

name

address

telephone

fax

name

address

telephone

fax

name

address

telephone

fax

name

address

telephone

fax

Jester

name

address

telephone

fax

name

address

telephone

fax

name

address

telephone

fax

name

address

telephone

fax

name

address

telephone

fax

name

address

telephone

fax

J

name ....

address ....

....

....

telephone ....

fax ....

name ....

address ....

....

....

telephone ....

fax ....

name ....

address ....

....

....

telephone ....

fax ....

name ....

address ....

....

....

telephone ....

fax ....

READ THIS IN THE MIRROR
BY THE LIGHT OF ANY MOON
SO THE FUTURE LIES BEHIND YOU
AND THE PAST WILL BE HERE SOON

Juggler

name ....
address ....
....
....
telephone ....
fax ....

name ....
address ....
....
....
telephone ....
fax ....

name ....
address ....
....
....
telephone ....
fax ....

name ....
address ....
....
....
telephone ....
fax ....

name ....
address ....
....
....
telephone ....
fax ....

name ....
address ....
....
....
telephone ....
fax ....

A cat that patrols Heathrow Airport
can juggle with duty-free wine,
    but try as he might
    with practice at night
    he still finds it hard
    to juggle with lard:
it's a technique he wants to refine.

Kiwi

name ....

address ....

....

....

telephone ....

fax ....

name ....

address ....

....

....

telephone ....

fax ....

name ....

address ....

....

....

telephone ....

fax ....

name ....

address ....

....

....

telephone ....

fax ....

a flightless bird called Faith
began to carry boulders:
for years she took these weights
strapped between her shoulders;
and as you might expect
the sweat poured like a fountain,
but only time will tell
if Faith can move a mountain.

K

name

address

telephone

fax

name

address

telephone

fax

name

address

telephone

fax

name

address

telephone

fax

name

address

telephone

fax

name

address

telephone

fax

What happened to
your last husband,
Mrs. Rodin?

name

address

telephone

fax

name

address

telephone

fax

name

address

telephone

fax

name

address

telephone

fax

K

name

address

telephone

fax

name

address

telephone

fax

name

address

telephone

fax

name

address

telephone

fax

Now, this is how
you fit a
contact lens

name ....

address ....

....

....

telephone ....

fax ....

name ....

address ....

....

....

telephone ....

fax ....

name ....

address ....

....

....

telephone ....

fax ....

name ....

address ....

....

....

telephone ....

fax ....

name ....

address ....

....

....

telephone ....

fax ....

name ....

address ....

....

....

telephone ....

fax ....

name

address

telephone

fax

name

address

telephone

fax

name

address

telephone

fax

name

address

telephone

fax

name

address

telephone

fax

name

address

telephone

fax

Lemming

name ....

address ....

....

....

telephone ....

fax ....

name ....

address ....

....

....

telephone ....

fax ....

name ....

address ....

....

....

telephone ....

fax ....

name ....

address ....

....

....

telephone ....

fax ....

name ....

address ....

....

....

telephone ....

fax ....

name ....

address ....

....

....

telephone ....

fax ....

L

lemming meringue pie

Moth

moth

name ....

address ....

....

....

telephone ....

fax ....

name ....

address ....

....

....

telephone ....

fax ....

name ....

address ....

....

....

telephone ....

fax ....

name ....

address ....

....

....

telephone ....

fax ....

name

address

telephone

fax

name

address

telephone

fax

motheaten

drew

name

address

telephone

fax

name

address

telephone

fax

Mollusc

name

address

telephone

fax

---

name

address

telephone

fax

---

name

address

telephone

fax

---

name

address

telephone

fax

---

name

address

telephone

fax

---

name

address

telephone

fax

molluse of the glen

name ....

address ....

....

....

telephone ....

fox ....

name ....

address ....

....

....

telephone ....

fox ....

Mole

name

address

telephone

fax

name

address

telephone

fax

name

address

telephone

fax

name

address

telephone

fax

name

address

telephone

fax

name

address

telephone

fax

M

name

address

telephone

fax

name

address

telephone

fax

MOLE OF KINTYRE

name

address

telephone

fax

name

address

telephone

fax

Nostra dormouse

name ....

address ....
....
....

telephone ....

fax ....

---

name ....

address ....
....
....

telephone ....

fax ....

---

name ....

address ....
....
....

telephone ....

fax ....

name ....

address ....
....
....

telephone ....

fax ....

---

name ....

address ....
....
....

telephone ....

fax ....

---

name ....

address ....
....
....

telephone ....

fax ....

nostra dormouse

Nelguin

nelguin

name ....

address ....

....

....

telephone ....

fax ....

---

name ....

address ....

....

....

telephone ....

fax ....

---

name ....

address ....

....

....

telephone ....

fax ....

---

name ....

address ....

....

....

telephone ....

fax ....

name

address

telephone

fax

name

address

telephone

fax

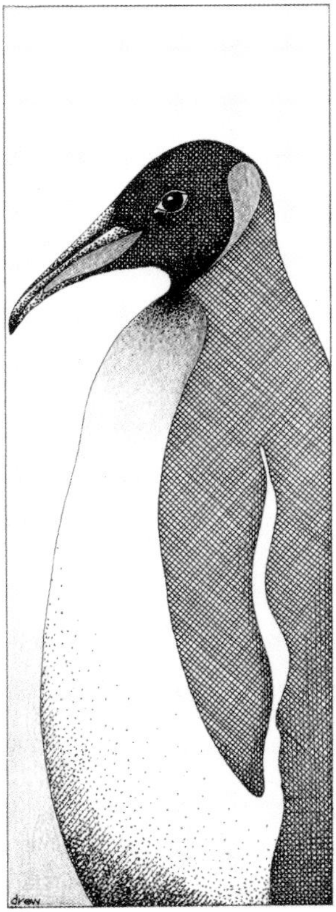

penguin

name

address

telephone

fax

name

address

telephone

fax

O for the wings of a dove

name

address

telephone

fax

---

name

address

telephone

fax

---

name

address

telephone

fax

---

name

address

telephone

fax

---

name

address

telephone

fax

---

name

address

telephone

fax

L for the lavender over the bed
M for the man that I love
N for the nasty bits stuck in the sink
O for the wings of a dove

name ....

address ....

....

....

telephone ....

fax ....

name ....

address ....

....

....

telephone ....

fax ....

name ....

address ....

....

....

telephone ....

fax ....

name ....

address ....

....

....

telephone ....

fax ....

name ....

address ....

....

....

telephone ....

fax ....

name ....

address ....

....

....

telephone ....

fax ....

O

name

address

telephone

fax

name

address

telephone

fax

name

address

telephone

fax

name

address

telephone

fax

name

address

telephone

fax

name

address

telephone

fax

st. francis talking at crossed porpoises

name

address

telephone

fax

name

address

telephone

fax

name

address

telephone

fax

name

address

telephone

fax

name

address

telephone

fax

name

address

telephone

fax

Pope

name

address

telephone

fax

---

name

address

telephone

fax

---

name

address

telephone

fax

---

name

address

telephone

fax

---

name

address

telephone

fax

---

name

address

telephone

fax

P

name

address

telephone

fox

name

address

telephone

fox

pope springs eternal

name

address

telephone

fox

name

address

telephone

fox

Puffin

PUFFIN

name ....

address ....

....

....

telephone ....

fax ....

name ....

address ....

....

....

telephone ....

fax ....

name ....

address ....

....

....

telephone ....

fax ....

name ....

address ....

....

....

telephone ....

fax ....

P

name

address

telephone

fox

name

address

telephone

fox

NUFFIN

name

address

telephone

fox

name

address

telephone

fox

Queen

name ....

address ....

....

....

telephone ....

fax ....

name ....

address ....

....

....

telephone ....

fax ....

name ....

address ....

....

....

telephone ....

fax ....

name ....

address ....

....

....

telephone ....

fax ....

name

address

telephone

fox

name

address

telephone

fox

name

address

telephone

fox

name

address

telephone

fox

name

address

telephone

fox

name

address

telephone

fox

Rake

name ....

address ....
....
....

telephone ....

fax ....

---

name ....

address ....
....
....

telephone ....

fax ....

---

name ....

address ....
....
....

telephone ....

fax ....

---

name ....

address ....
....
....

telephone ....

fax ....

---

name ....

address ....
....
....

telephone ....

fax ....

---

name ....

address ....
....
....

telephone ....

fax ....

R

name

address

telephone

fax

name

address

telephone

fax

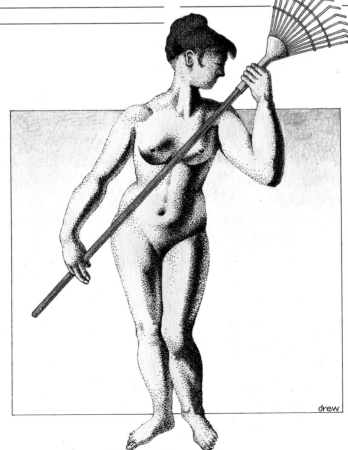

drew

the rake of the sabine women

Reindeer

name ....

address ....

....

....

telephone ....

fax ....

name ....

address ....

....

....

telephone ....

fax ....

name ....

address ....

....

....

telephone ....

fax ....

name ....

address ....

....

....

telephone ....

fax ....

name ....

address ....

....

....

telephone ....

fax ....

name ....

address ....

....

....

telephone ....

fax ....

R

name

address

telephone

fax

name

address

telephone

fax

Last christmas Papa bought a reindeer,
to pull our toboggan, he said.
But it rained for the whole of december
so it played the piano instead.

name

address

telephone

fax

name

address

telephone

fax

Rats

name ....

address ....
....
....

telephone ....

fax ....

---

name ....

address ....
....
....

telephone ....

fax ....

---

name ....

address ....
....
....

telephone ....

fax ....

---

name ....

address ....
....
....

telephone ....

fax ....

---

name ....

address ....
....
....

telephone ....

fax ....

---

name ....

address ....
....
....

telephone ....

fax ....

R

Sheep

name

address

telephone

fax

name

address

telephone

fax

name

address

telephone

fax

name

address

telephone

fax

name

address

telephone

fax

name

address

telephone

fax

name

address

telephone

fax

name

address

telephone

fax

....and all I ask is a tall sheep....
....and a star to steer her by.

name

address

telephone

fax

name

address

telephone

fax

Sickert

name

address

telephone

fax

---

name

address

telephone

fax

---

name

address

telephone

fax

---

name

address

telephone

fax

---

name

address

telephone

fax

---

name

address

telephone

fax

sickert as a parrot

$\mathcal{S}$hip

First of all you fetch some paper
wood and bits of string:
then construct the perfect schooner,
strength must be the thing.

Now a bottle: this is crucial.
Don't pick one too thin.
If you're making something special
choose one made for gin.

name ....

address ....

....

....

telephone ....

fax ....

---

name ....

address ....

....

....

telephone ....

fax ....

---

name ....

address ....

....

....

telephone ....

fax ....

name

address

telephone

fax

name

address

telephone

fax

name

address

telephone

fax

But this bottle must be empty
(letting in the boat).
Place the contents in a tumbler
then transfer to throat.

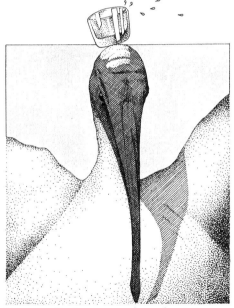

Now you'll sing a rousing chorus
as you dance a jig;
(though the ship's not in the bottle
you won't give a fig).

T

name

address

telephone

fax

---

name

address

telephone

fax

---

name

address

telephone

fax

---

name

address

telephone

fax

---

name

address

telephone

fax

---

name

address

telephone

fax

name ....

address ....

....

....

telephone ....

fax ....

name ....

address ....

....

....

telephone ....

fax ....

name ....

address ....

....

....

telephone ....

fax ....

name ....

address ....

....

....

telephone ....

fax ....

THOSE DARK SATANIC
MOLES

Tutu

name

address

telephone

fax

---

name

address

telephone

fax

---

name

address

telephone

fax

---

name

address

telephone

fax

---

name

address

telephone

fax

---

name

address

telephone

fax

name ....

address ....

....

....

telephone ....

fax ....

name ....

address ....

....

....

telephone ....

fax ....

dodo in a tutu
in a haha

name ....

address ....

....

....

telephone ....

fax ....

name ....

address ....

....

....

telephone ....

fax ....

Three

name

address

telephone

fax

---

name

address

telephone

fax

---

name

address

telephone

fax

---

name

address

telephone

fax

---

name

address

telephone

fax

---

name

address

telephone

fax

the love of three orang utans

name ....

address ....

....

....

telephone ....

fax ....

name ....

address ....

....

....

telephone ....

fax ....

T

name

address

telephone

fax

---

name

address

telephone

fax

---

name

address

telephone

fax

---

name

address

telephone

fax

---

name

address

telephone

fax

---

name

address

telephone

fax

name

address

telephone

fax

name

address

telephone

fax

name

address

telephone

fax

name

address

telephone

fax

name

address

telephone

fax

name

address

telephone

fax

Tuba

name

address

telephone

fax

---

name

address

telephone

fax

---

name

address

telephone

fax

---

name

address

telephone

fax

---

name

address

telephone

fax

---

name

address

telephone

fax

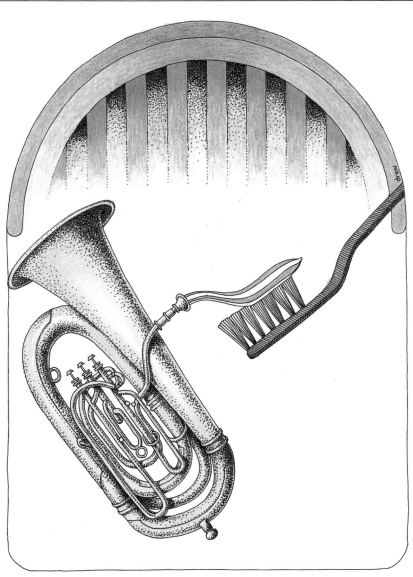

tuba toothpaste

U

name

address

telephone

fax

name

address

telephone

fax

name

address

telephone

fax

name

address

telephone

fax

name

address

telephone

fax

name

address

telephone

fax

U

name

address

telephone

fax

name

address

telephone

fax

name

address

telephone

fax

name

address

telephone

fax

name

address

telephone

fax

name

address

telephone

fax

U

name

address

telephone

fax

name

address

telephone

fax

name

address

telephone

fax

name

address

telephone

fax

name

address

telephone

fax

name

address

telephone

fax

name ....

address ....

....

....

telephone ....

fax ....

name ....

address ....

....

....

telephone ....

fax ....

name ....

address ....

....

telephone ....

fax ....

The sun is setting and nobody cares;
the evening has caught them all unawares.
The ploughman returns to his block of flats:
he's putting the pigeon among the cats.

Upside-down peacock horse

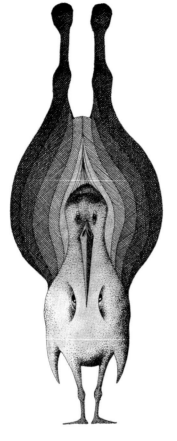

name ....

address ....

....

....

telephone ....

fax ....

name ....

address ....

....

....

telephone ....

fax ....

It is not generally known that the horse evolved from the peacock: this bird used to have the curious habit of landing upside down on its tail feathers. A few birds of the species stayed this way up and passed the characteristic on to their offspring. Illustrated here is the intermediary species which is capable of remaining in either position:

woken from a distant dream
with a sudden jerk
sitting in an onion patch
garden spirits lurk
humming tunes to soothe you, with
music while you work.

Venus

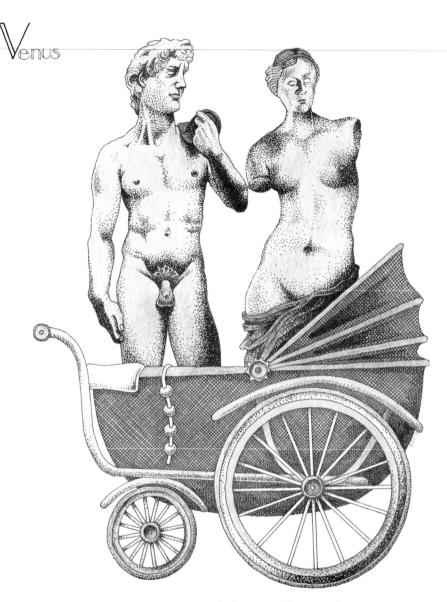

When David met Venus de Milo
it seemed such a harmless affair
but the offspring were little fat cherubs
that had to be put into care.
And when these grew older and virile
they fathered some more of their own;

V

name

address

telephone

fax

name

address

telephone

fax

name

address

telephone

fax

name

address

telephone

fax

name

address

telephone

fax

name

address

telephone

fax

Wolfgang

name

address

telephone

fax

---

name

address

telephone

fax

---

name

address

telephone

fax

---

name

address

telephone

fax

---

name

address

telephone

fax

---

name

address

telephone

fax

W

wolf gang mows art

Wayne

name

address

telephone

fax

---

name

address

telephone

fax

---

name

address

telephone

fax

---

name

address

telephone

fax

---

name

address

telephone

fax

---

name

address

telephone

fax

W

The moon was full as the Messerschmidt soared
and Kevin played with his parachute cord;
Tracey was taking her pilot's test
and Wayne flew over the cuckoo's nest.

name ....

address ....

....

....

telephone ....

fax ....

name ....

address ....

....

....

telephone ....

fax ....

Whiting

name ....

address ....

....

....

telephone ....

fax ....

name ....

address ....

....

....

telephone ....

fax ....

name ....

address ....

....

....

telephone ....

fax ....

name ....

address ....

....

....

telephone ....

fax ....

name ....

address ....

....

....

telephone ....

fax ....

name ....

address ....

....

....

telephone ....

fax ....

joined up whiting

---

name..

address...

....

....

telephone..

fax..

---

name..

address...

....

....

telephone..

fax..

Waders

name

address

telephone

fax

waders

name

address

telephone

fax

name

address

telephone

fax

name

address

telephone

fax

name

address

telephone

fax

name

address

telephone

fax

name

address

telephone

fax

name

address

telephone

fax

name

address

telephone

fax

name

address

telephone

fax

name

address

telephone

fax

double yellow lions

drew

name

address

telephone

fax

name

address

telephone

fax

name

address

telephone

fax

name

address

telephone

fax

name

address

telephone

fax

name

address

telephone

fax

Y

name

address

telephone

fax

name

address

telephone

fax

name

address

telephone

fax

name

address

telephone

fax

name

address

telephone

fax

name

address

telephone

fax

zadok: the piste

name ....

address ....

....

....

telephone ....

fax ....

name ....

address ....

....

....

telephone ....

fax ....

Z

name ....

address ....

....

....

telephone ....

fax ....

---

name ....

address ....

....

....

telephone ....

fax ....

---

name ....

address ....

....

....

telephone ....

fax ....

name ....

address ....

....

....

telephone ....

fax ....

---

name ....

address ....

....

....

telephone ....

fax ....

---

name ....

address ....

....

....

telephone ....

fax ....

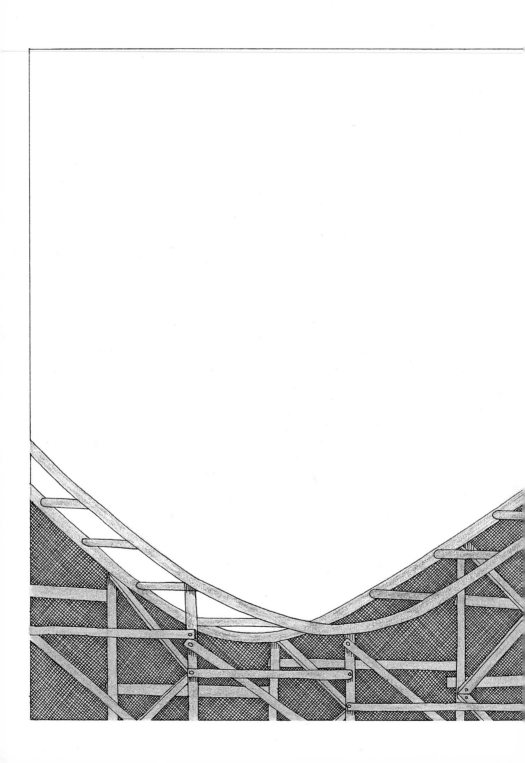